PRESENTED TO:

_____

FROM:

_____

DATE:

_____

© 2019 by Thomas Nelson

Material from this book was drawn from *Grateful for You*, © 2014 Thomas Nelson, ISBN 978-0-529-12186-8.

All rights reserved. No portion of this book may be reproduced, stored in a retrieval system, or transmitted in any form or by any means—electronic, mechanical, photocopy, recording, scanning, or other—except for brief quotations in critical reviews or articles, without the prior written permission of the publisher.

Published in Nashville, Tennessee, by Thomas Nelson. Thomas Nelson is a registered trademark of HarperCollins Christian Publishing, Inc.

Thomas Nelson titles may be purchased in bulk for educational, business, fundraising, or sales promotional use. For information, please email SpecialMarkets@ ThomasNelson.com.

Unless otherwise noted, Scripture quotations are taken from the Holy Bible, New International Version®, NIV®. Copyright © 1973, 1978, 1984, 2011 by Biblica, Inc.™ Used by permission of Zondervan. All rights reserved worldwide. www.zondervan. com. The "NIV" and "New International Version" are trademarks registered in the United States Patent and Trademark Office by Biblica, Inc.™

Scripture quotations marked ESV are taken from the ESV® Bible (The Holy Bible, English Standard Version®). Copyright © 2001 by Crossway, a publishing ministry of Good News Publishers. Used by permission. All rights reserved.

Scripture quotations marked MSG are taken from *The Message*. Copyright © by Eugene H. Peterson 1993, 1994, 1995, 1996, 2000, 2001, 2002. Used by permission of NavPress. All rights reserved. Represented by Tyndale House Publishers, Inc.

Scripture quotations marked NLT are taken from the Holy Bible, New Living Translation. © 1996, 2004, 2007, 2013, 2015 by Tyndale House Foundation. Used by permission of Tyndale House Publishers, Inc., Carol Stream, Illinois 60188. All rights reserved.

Scripture quotations marked KJV are taken from the King James Version.

Scripture quotations marked NASB are taken from New American Standard Bible®, Copyright © 1960, 1962, 1963, 1968, 1971, 1972, 1973, 1975, 1977, 1995 by The Lockman Foundation. Used by permission. (www.Lockman.org)

Scripture quotations marked TLB are taken from The Living Bible. Copyright © 1971. Used by permission of Tyndale House Publishers, Inc., Carol Stream, Illinois 60188. All rights reserved.

Any Internet addresses, phone numbers, or company or product information printed in this book are offered as a resource and are not intended in any way to be or to imply an endorsement by Thomas Nelson, nor does Thomas Nelson vouch for the existence, content, or services of these sites, phone numbers, companies, or products beyond the life of this book.

ISBN (HC): 978-1-4002-0908-8
ISBN (eBook): 978-1-4002-0936-1

Printed in China

19 20 21 22 23 GRI 10 9 8 7 6 5 4 3 2 1

THANKFUL
for YOU

THOMAS NELSON
Since 1798

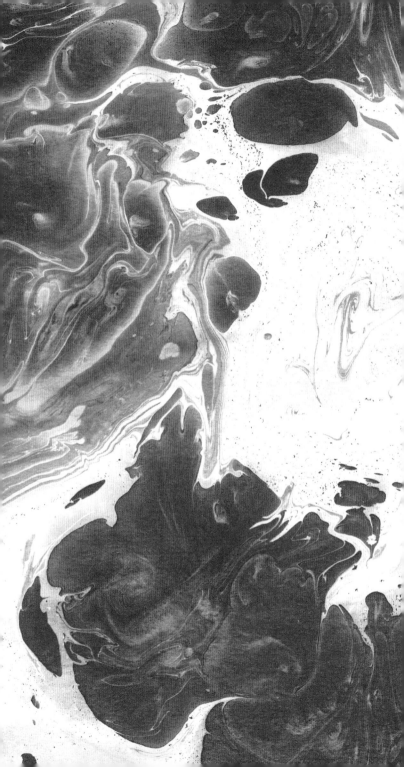

INTRODUCTION

"I'm so grateful for you—you have no idea." "I appreciate you more than you know." "You're the best friend I've ever had."

While we often say these things, they don't always express the depth of meaning we want to convey. After all, a faithful friend is priceless! *Thankful for You* is a beautiful celebration of friendship that relays our profound love and gratefulness for friends' presence in our lives.

Some of the quotations in this book inspire deeper friendships; some declare the glories of a trusting, giving relationship; some announce gratitude for faithful companions. All affirm the wonders of true friends and how blessed they make us feel.

We can see in Scripture that friendship was God's idea. Consider the heartfelt pact Jonathan made with David: "We have sworn loyalty to each other in the LORD's name. The LORD is the witness of a bond between us and our children forever" (1 Samuel 20:42 NLT). Witness Ruth's determination never to forsake her widowed mother-in-law: "Wherever you go, I will go; wherever you live, I will live. Your people will be my people, and your God will be my God" (Ruth 1:16 NLT). And finally, see how Paul praised Epaphroditus: "He is a true brother, co-worker, and fellow soldier. . . . Give him the honor that people like him deserve" (Philippians 2:25, 29 NLT).

Good friends deserve honor. As you read, enjoy these facets of friendships and the loving ways they bring grace and gladness to your life.

Agree with
each other,
love each other, be
deep-spirited
friends.

—Philippians 2:2 MSG

It is in the shelter
of each other that
people live.

—Irish proverb

Friendship is the only cement that will ever hold the world together.

—Woodrow T. Wilson

Love from the
center of who
you are. . . . Be
good friends who
love deeply.

—Romans 12:9–10 MSG

He who placed the stars

in the heavens placed you

in my life . . . and I am

truly grateful.

The one who
blesses others is
abundantly blessed;
those who help
others are helped.

—Proverbs 11:25 MSG

No friendship

is an accident.

—O. Henry

Every time you

cross my mind,

I break out in

exclamations of

thanks to God.

—Philippians 1:3 MSG

My friend, I pray that you "will be filled with fresh joy from the LORD."

—Isaiah 29:19 NLT

When I think of

people who have

made a difference in

my life, you quickly

come to mind.

Real friendship is shown

in times of trouble.

Prosperity is full of friends.

—Euripides

The pleasantness
of a friend
springs from their
heartfelt advice.

—Proverbs 27:9

Gratitude is the memory
of the heart.

—Jean-Baptiste Massieu

When you have been

through hard times

and come out the other

side, look around you.

The people still there

are your true friends.

I'm thankful you have

been there for me.

This is the day
that the Lord
has made; let
us rejoice and
be glad in it.

—Psalm 118:24 ESV

Today I rejoice in my

gratitude for you!

One universe,

8 planets,

7 seas, . . .

and I had the privilege

to meet you.

I thank my God

always when I

remember you

in my prayers.

—Philemon 1:4 ESV

At times our own light goes out and is rekindled by a spark from another person. Each of us has cause to think with deep gratitude of those who have lighted the flame within us.

—Albert Schweitzer

Oh, the comfort—the inexpressible comfort of feeling safe with a person— having neither to weigh thoughts nor measure words, but pouring them all right out, just as they are, chaff and grain together; knowing that a faithful hand will take and sift them, keep what is worth keeping, and then with the breath of kindness blow the rest away.

—Dinah Maria Mulock Craik

Let us love one
another: for love
is of God.

—1 John 4:7 KJV

It is not joy that

makes us grateful.

It is gratitude that

makes us joyful.

To have a good
friend is one of life's
greatest delights; to be
a good friend, one of the
noblest undertakings.

—Unknown

As we grow up we

realize it is less

important to have

lots of friends and

more important to

have real ones.

Thank you for

being real.

There is nothing on this earth more to be prized than true friendship.

—Thomas Aquinas

One friend

sharpens another.

—Proverbs 27:17 MSG

It may be true that he

travels farthest who

travels alone, but the

goal thus reached is

not worth reaching.

—Theodore Roosevelt

I'm so thankful to be traveling with you.

The highest privilege

is the privilege of

being allowed to

share another's life.

However rare true love
may be, it is less so than
true friendship.

—François de La Rochefoucauld

You talk about your

pleasures with your

acquaintances; you

talk about your troubles

with your friends.

Every good
and perfect
gift is
from above.

—James 1:17

You are a beautiful gift to me.

A friend is someone

who knows all about you

and still loves you.

—Elbert Hubbard

Friendship isn't a big thing;

it's a million little things.

Kindred spirits are not so scarce as I used to think. It's splendid to find out there are so many of them in the world.

—L. M. Montgomery,
Anne of Green Gables

How good you make others

feel about themselves

says a lot about you.

*Dear Lord, thank
You for friends whose
kindness spills over
into others' lives.
Please help me to
be more like my
friend—loving, giving,
thoughtful—a humble
reflection of You.*

The time you've given and

the wisdom you've shared

have blessed me.

True friendship is a plant
of slow growth, and must
undergo and withstand the
shocks of adversity before it is
entitled to the appellation.

—George Washington

There is always, always,

always something to

be thankful for. You are

that person for me.

He fills my life with
good things.

—Psalm 103:5 NLT

Words are easy,
like the wind;
Faithful friends are
hard to find.

—William Shakespeare,
The Passionate Pilgrim

O Lord, what a privilege to live knowing that we are Your children! Thank You for seeing fit to save us and love us with an incomparable love, so that we might love one another.

Friendship multiplies the good
of life and divides the evil.

—Baltasar Gracián

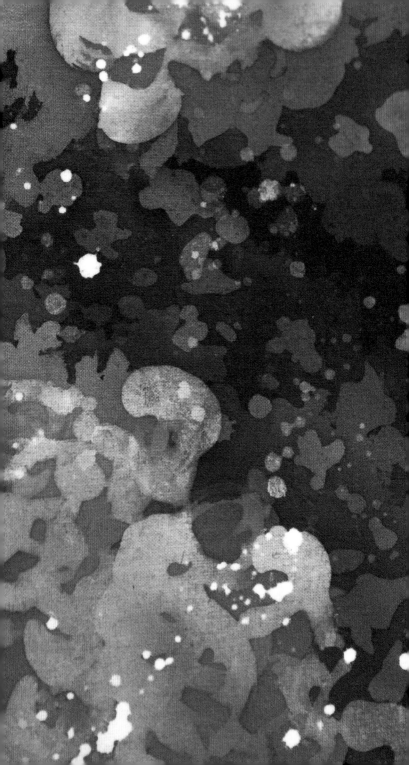

The sincere friends of this world are as ship lights in the stormiest of nights.

—Giotto di Bondone

There is nothing that
makes us love someone so
much as praying for them.

—William Law

May you be richly

rewarded by the

LORD, the God of

Israel, under whose

wings you . . .

take refuge.

—Ruth 2:12

Good friends are among our greatest blessings—they may keep us back from much evil, quicken us in our course, speak a word in season, draw us upward, and draw us on.

—J. C. Ryle

A kind deed from a friend

is a gift from God.

I have not
stopped thanking
God for you.

—Ephesians 1:16 NLT

The worship most acceptable
to God comes from a thankful
and cheerful heart.

—Plutarch

Sing to the LORD

with grateful praise;

make music to our

God on the harp.

—Psalm 147:7

How truly is a kind heart a fountain

of gladness, making everything in

its vicinity to freshen into smiles.

—Washington Irving

Your friendship is a

source of great joy.

Let us be grateful to the people who make us happy; they are the charming gardeners who make our souls blossom.

—Marcel Proust

Let your roots grow
down into him, and let
your lives be built on
him. Then your faith
will grow strong in the
truth you were taught,
and you will overflow
with thankfulness.

—Colossians 2:7 NLT

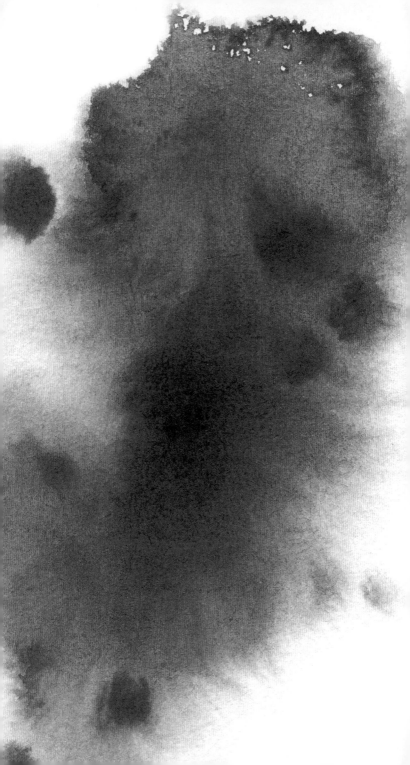

Every now and then it's good

to pause in our pursuit of

happiness and just be happy.

I'm so happy to know you.

Love is flower-like;

friendship is

a sheltering tree.

—Samuel Taylor Coleridge

May he give you the

desire of your heart

and make all your

plans succeed.

—Psalm 20:4

One of the most beautiful
qualities of true friendship is to
understand and to be understood.

—Lucius Annaeus Seneca

I'm so grateful that
one of the lives you've
touched is mine.

Good friends laugh,
cry, and encourage
each other. But most
important, true
friends point one
another to Jesus.

I find myself
praying for you
with a glad heart.

—Philippians 1:4 MSG

Dear heavenly Father,

thank You for placing

someone in my life

who points me to

You . . . who spurs

me to live in a way

that pleases You.

I pray that I can be

more like this dear

one in imitating and

glorifying You.

May the Lord
continually bless
you with heaven's
blessings as well as
with human joys.

—Psalm 128:5 TLB

There is nothing I would
not do for those who are
really my friends. I have no
notion of loving people by
halves; it is not my nature.

—Jane Austen, *Northanger Abbey*

Each time

you come to

mind I think,

Thank You,

Lord, for such

a dear friend.

In everything give thanks; for this is God's will for you in Christ Jesus.

—1 Thessalonians 5:18 NASB

Laughter is not a

bad beginning for a

friendship, and it is the

best ending for one.

—Henry Ward Beecher

Above all, keep
loving one another
earnestly, since love
covers a multitude
of sins. Show
hospitality. . . . As
each has received a
gift, use it to serve
one another, as
good stewards.

—1 Peter 4:8–10 ESV

Hold a true friend with

both your hands.

—Nigerian proverb

If I had a flower for every time I thought of you . . . I could walk through my garden forever.

—Alfred, Lord Tennyson

Light is sweet, and
it is pleasant for the
eyes to see the sun.

—Ecclesiastes 11:7 ESV

You beam a lovely brightness into my heart.

I'm grateful to have

you in my life.

Mercy, peace and love be yours in abundance.

—Jude 1:2

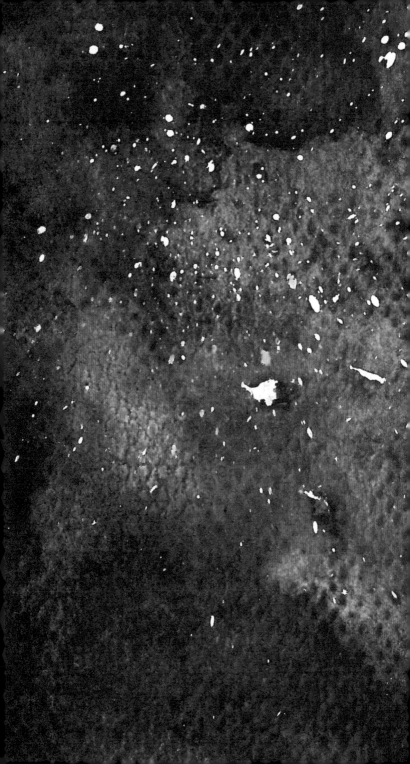

*I pray God multiplies
back to you the blessing you
are many times over.*

The glory of friendship is not the outstretched hand, not the kindly smile, nor the joy of companionship; it is the spiritual inspiration that comes to one when you discover that someone else believes in you and is willing to trust you with a friendship.

—Ralph Waldo Emerson

The blessing of the LORD be on you.

—Psalm 129:8

A friend is a gift you
give yourself.

—Robert Louis Stevenson

I have perceiv'd that to be

with those I like is enough.

—Walt Whitman

Two people are better off than one, for they can help each other succeed. If one person falls, the other can reach out and help. But someone who falls alone is in real trouble.

—Ecclesiastes 4:9–10 NLT